On the Other Hand

Improve your tennis game by giving your
non-dominant hand its own special role

Scott Wilson Nichols

Photography by Al Risebrow and Brady Nichols

Foreword by Nicholas A. DiNubile, MD
*Orthopedic surgeon, best-selling author of FrameWork,
and USPTA member*

• • • •

Published by Nichols Pro Publishing
www.snicholspro.com
San Juan Capistrano, California USA

Produced by Lookbook Press
Seattle, Washington USA

ISBN 978-0-615-59579-5

Library of Congress 2012931809

Printed in USA

• • • •

Acknowledgements

From Scott,

Many thanks to my parents, Lynne and John Nichols for getting me started in tennis; to brother John and sister Cyndy for their ever lasting support; to my wife Colleen, her parents Gerald and Rosemary and my daughter Marissa and son Brady for their love and help with this book; to my personal friends over the years; Stacy, Ross, Skip, Cesar, Smith, Scott, Tut, Bobby, David, Linda, Mike, Bryce, and Marc. Lastly, to my professional mentors; Peter Young, Woody Hunt, John Meeks and Kurt Kamperman; without all of you, this book would not of happened.

It is my hope that this book will aid many players of all ages and abilities, as well as, providing coaches and pros another tool in promoting the role of the non-dominant arm, as they teach tennis strokes to their students.

Table of Contents

Foreword

I've had the fortune to work with many professional and high level athletes over the years. In addition to their hard work and dedication, there is another common thread that binds them. Their work all too often appears effortless, and they almost never look off balance. High speed biomechanical analysis has helped explain this phenomenon and consistently captures very specific movement patterns, whether they are hitting a slap shot, driving a golf ball or hitting a winner down the line.

Effective sport biomechanics is not about any one body part carrying the load, but rather an orchestrated effort by the entire body, from floor to core....and more. One only has to watch my all-time favorite athlete, Roger Federer, to appreciate the human body working efficiently and in concert. His precision Swiss movement involves not only his hitting arm but also his non-dominant arm, which actually plays a pretty dominant role in ensuring his predictable shot making. This is true of all of his strokes, be it his legendary forehand, his volleys, or even his variety of backhands. His non-dominant arm, although not the lead actor, plays a critical supporting role helping to guide his movement patterns, his biomechanics, to his usual successful outcome. And it's not just Roger. Watch any top player and you'll witness the same effective use of the "other" arm. "On the Other Hand" tackles this very topic in a way that will have you using your whole body more effectively and efficiently, as you become a more complete tennis player.

I first met Scott Nichols at a USPTA conference in La Quinta, California. We played some tennis, talked a lot, and kept in touch afterward. I was very impressed with Scott's depth of knowledge not only about the game, but more importantly about the biomechanics of optimal stroke production and the critical role the non-dominant arm plays in that regard. I was thrilled to hear that Scott was working on a book centered on this very issue. Scott has enjoyed many successes in the world of tennis, both on and off the court. As a player he is well-known and well-liked, and has won numerous USTA national championships among the other impressive achievements. As a teaching pro he is helped countless individuals play better, win championships and have more fun with this wonderful lifetime sport.

In "On the Other Hand," Scott shares his wealth of knowledge in an easy-to-read, easy to implement format. His practical teaching skills come through loud and clear as if he were on the court with you. This book is different than any tennis instruction book I have ever seen in that its focus is the non-dominant arm, but it doesn't end there. In addition to his insights on effective use of the non-dominant arm, and how it is critical in racquet preparation, accuracy and control, Scott shares numerous other practical tips that will improve your game. As an orthopedic surgeon, I can tell you without doubt that the far majority of the tennis related injuries and ailments I see, especially in the nonprofessional, are rooted in technical flaws. Proper biomechanics is the key not only to winning tennis, but also to injury prevention, especially those nagging recurrent ones, and Scott's information will go a long way in keeping you out of my office.

"On the Other Hand" is a must read for any tennis enthusiast but is targeted to beginner and intermediate players hoping to improve their skills and get to the next level. Instructors and coaches will also learn many pearls of wisdom that can be shared with their students. I am glad to have "On the Other Hand" in my arsenal, and you will be too.

Nicholas A. DiNubile, MD
Orthopedic surgeon, best-selling author of FrameWork, and USPTA member

About the Author

Scott Wilson Nichols, is currently, the Director of Tennis at the prestigious Marbella Country Club in San Juan Capistrano, California. Prior to this position, Scott served as Director of Tennis at Long Cove Club on Hilton Head Island, South Carolina. While on Hilton Head Island, he was also the Hilton Head Island High School Tennis Coach for the boys/girls tennis teams and the girls were state champions in 2007-2010.

Scott competes on the USTA National Senior Circuit and plays adult state and regional 5.0 team tennis. Over the course of his

playing career, Scott has been consistently ranked state wide, regionally and nationally, as well as, internationally. ITF # 23 Internationally and # 1 Nationally were his highest rankings. In 2005, Nichols was named United States Professional Tennis Association (USPTA) Southern Division 35 and over Player of the Year and also, was awarded the prestigious Professional Tennis Registry USPTR player of the year. In 2004, Nichols was selected by the USTA committee, as a member of the United States Trabert Cup Team, traveling to Turkey to compete for the United States. On the road to success, Nichols attended Guilford College in Greensboro, North Carolina, where he played four years of varsity tennis. At age 18, he won the Eastern Section Junior Grass Court Singles Championship. Twenty-five years later, in 2003, he won the USTA National Men's 40s Grass Court Tennis Championship. Scott has won 6 USTA National tennis balls.

Nichols' goal in this book is to affect the world of tennis beyond the local and regional level by introducing players, tennis instructors and tennis coaches of all abilities to a proven technique that is broadly used in the amateur and pro ranks, but rarely taught–the role of the non-dominant hand in all tennis strokes.

Hilton Head Island High School Boys Tennis Team 2009-2010 Regional Champions

Hilton Head Island High School Girls Tennis Team 2010 Defending State Champions (2007-2010)

About the Photographers

Al Risebrow started his tennis teaching career soon after attending his first year of college and taught for many years at a variety of clubs on the North Shore of Long Island, NY while at the same time playing in local tournaments. After earning enough money for professional camera equipment, he started shooting pictures on a professional basis and it wasn't long before he directed his talents to taking photographs of professional and amateur tennis players. While fashion photography captured  his interest for a short while, it was really the law that he wanted to pursue. Today, while he still plays tennis and takes photographs, he is a practicing lawyer specializing in professional and general liability defense litigation for a variety of clients primarily in New York City.

Brady Nichols, my son, always enjoyed watching his dad compete and personally, enjoyed playing doubles in USTA Jr. Tournaments with Trey Hale, being a member of the Boy's Hilton Head Island High School Team for 5 years and lastly, competing on the HHI Jr.  Team Tennis League. Throughout his junior and high school years, Brady became involved with taking pictures with his grandfather Gerald and also, was a staff photographer for the High School yearbook. This new love and possible future career 'rocketed' off to Brady receiving several awards and recognition for his photography and art, which lead to Brady entering college at Winthrop University in 2010 as a Photography/ Art Major. He enjoyed helping his dad with this book and looks forward to possibly writing his own some day.

Preface

Everybody's doing it, but no one is talking about it: using the non-dominant hand in tennis! Have you ever watched Andy Roddick propel himself through a shot as if he's going to follow the ball right over the net? That kind of power doesn't come from the racquet alone. It comes from total body involvement, and that includes giving the non-dominant hand its own important role to play.

I'm Scott Nichols, and I've been studying the use of the non-dominant hand for over 15 years. By emulating other professionals and adding these techniques to my own game, I've discovered a whole new dimension of tennis. By sharing this information with you, I hope to influence the way the game is taught and ultimately the way it is played.

Who can benefit from this book?

Whether you are a teaching pro, coach, tournament, recreational or wheelchair player, you can take your game to the next level by learning to use your non-dominant hand. Granted, there are many playing styles and ways to produce each stroke. But the role of the non-dominant hand remains the same for every player, working in tandem with the racquet hand for balance, for measuring and for power. No matter who you are, to be a truly complete player, instructor or coach, you must be fully aware of the non-dominant hand and the role it plays in producing the most effective shots.

The good news is, anyone can learn the techniques presented here. It's not rocket science, but it's sound advice, based on the physical dynamics of the game of tennis. Regardless of your style or level of play, the use of the non-dominant hand is a tool that can help you improve every shot.

How is this book different?

No other book on the market covers the use of the non-dominant hand except in the most general sense. Maybe they don't want you to know the secret. Or maybe they assume that you'll figure it out on your own. I spell it out, offering you a fresh look at every stroke and a way to improve every shot.

How to use this book

This book is written and illustrated from a right-handed player's perspective. If you are a lefty, you'll need to think in reverse.

This book is a supplement to, not a substitute for professional instruction. Beginners will find some helpful grip, stroke and strategy tips, but may need professional guidance in the initial development of basic skills and good form. Our emphasis here is on the use of the non-dominant hand to improve your strokes and advance your game to a new level.

This is not another instruction manual to live on your bookshelf and collect dust. If you are an instructor or coach, use it as a guide for your lesson plans, practice sessions and pre-match preparations. If you are a player who wants to improve your game (and who doesn't?), take this book out on the practice court. Keep it in your racquet bag as a handy reference. Study the illustrations, and picture yourself going through the motions. Practice, practice, practice!

If you want to improve your tennis game, don't just let your non-dominant hand hang around. Give it a job and get ready for your best tennis yet. The secret is out: It's On the Other Hand.

Chapter 1

The Forehand Groundstroke

In singles or doubles play, the forehand groundstroke can be your weapon of mass destruction, helping you off-balance your opponent and set yourself up to move in for the kill. In this chapter, we'll talk about how you can most effectively use the basic groundstroke, when to add topspin or slice, what to do when you don't have time to step into the ball, and most importantly, how to use your non-dominant hand to add more power and control to every shot.

Get ready, get set

Whether you are driving the ball with power or adding topspin or slice, the key is getting into position. The basic position for hitting a successful forehand ground-stroke involves squaring your body to the ball and getting the racquet back. Ideally, the butt of the racquet should face the net and the head should face the back fence.

As you anticipate the ball coming to your forehand, the non-dominant arm extends loosely out to the point where you would like to meet the ball. As it travels to you, whether it is where you want it to be or you have to move to get in position for optimum reach of the hitting zone, use the non-dominant arm as a site, reaching your hand out as if to catch the ball. By doing so, the non-dominant hand becomes your instrument for balance, measuring and optimum power and torque.

To spin or not to spin?

In recent years, much emphasis has been put on generating top spin. The pros do it with extreme grips and outrageous swings. Whether you are an aspiring professional player, a teaching professional, a tournament player or recreational player, a little spin can go a long way in improving your forehand groundstroke.

Whether hitting a flat shot or adding topspin, the motion of the swing is low to high from your prepared position. For a driving power shot, the swing starts out level, finishing high.

The butt of the racquet faces the net;
catch the racquet on follow-through.

On the other hand

Here's where your non-dominant hand comes into play. As you swing low to high, like a plane taking off, position your non-dominant hand as if you might be throwing a Frisbee. Rotate both arms and shoulders as you step into the ball and swing, using the non-dominant hand as your measuring guide and to stabilize the swing.

Catch the racquet with your non-dominant hand, which is upward and way out in front. Now you've got the power!

Tip:

The Frisbee motion is key when you run around your backhand. Whether you hit cross court, down the middle or down the line, by throwing your body into the swing, you get maximum torque and momentum. Swing as fast as you physically can!

Note that the butt of the racquet starts out facing the net and finishes facing the net on the follow-through.

Topping it off

Want to gain control and add drama? Add topspin to your forehand groundstroke. Set up the same way you would for a flat stroke, square to the ball. From your ready position, as the ball approaches, concentrate on the back surface of the ball. Position the racquet lower than the ball, swinging faster and brushing up the back of the ball. Swing speed is key.

Racquet preparation for the topspin . . . forehand starts low; the non-dominant hand is waiting to play catch.

On the other hand

Your non-dominant arm is just dying to get into the action here. Use it like a propeller, throwing a huge amount of torque and effort into the upward, more vertical swing, following through with the racquet clearly across the body and around the opposite ear.

Slicing it up

Another control device you can add to your forehand arsenal is the slice, sometimes called a backspin or underspin shot. Is it for everybody? Yes. The slice is fairly easy to learn. But it's not a replacement for your flat or topspin groundstroke. Use the slice as:

- a defensive groundstroke or lob
- an approach shot to get to the net
- a surprise drop shot.

Slicing the ball will keep it low as it crosses the net and will cause the ball to bounce low, often forcing your opponent to scramble to get to it, compelling him to hit up on the ball.

Preparation for the shot is the same except that the racquet head starts high and the backswing is more compact and vertical. The racquet head does not need to face the fence on the backswing, but should be in about a 4 o'clock position.

Here's where it gets a little tricky. You must switch your brain to think the opposite from the topspin swing motion. Instead of hitting low to high, the slice requires a high-to-low swing, keeping a firm wrist, with the strings brushing downward on the back of ball.

On the other hand:

For this shot, the non-dominant hand is moving in tandem with the racquet hand, as if wearing handcuffs as you meet the ball. (No Frisbee throwing here!) Use it as an aid for balance and movement to the area where you would like to hit the ball. Exercise restraint on the follow-through and think "control." The non-dominant hand moves forward, and if you're good—really good—it should criss-cross over the racquet hand to finish. This is an advanced move and will take practice.

Putting your best foot forward

Life is grand when you have plenty of time to get to the ball and set up for your forehand groundstroke, turning your body and stepping into the ball with your left foot. But let's face it. The world inside the court lines is rarely perfect. Realistically, there will be many times when the best you can do is get to the ball on time to swing.

This is why you see so many of the pros on television using a more open stance. New racquet technology, increasing swing speeds and mega topspin add up to make it nearly impossible to set up for ground strokes in a traditional way.

You can still make the most of your shot in an open stance with your feet. It's what goes on above the waist that counts. Ready? Face the net like a goalie with your legs in an open stance V. As your racquet goes back in preparation to swing, your upper torso should be square to the ball.

On the other hand

Just as you used your non-dominant hand in your closed stance, it becomes even more critical from the open stance, helping to assure that your upper torso is turned. For this to happen in the game it takes constant practice.

Chapter 2

The Forehand Volley

Whether you are playing singles or doubles, the forehand volley is an aggressive shot—one which requires quick reflexes and stealth reaction. Because you have less time to set up for a shot from the net or from the mid-court "hot spot" position than you would for a ground stroke, the use of the non-dominant hand becomes even more critical. In this chapter, we'll talk about preparation for the volley, body alignment, grip choices, and court position. You'll get tips on and how to gain directional control and get the most power and pop from every volley.

Ready or not...

Preparation and positioning are crucial when you are at the net. Get ready to execute the perfect forehand volley by making sure you are in the ideal position:

- Feet facing the net, about shoulder width apart

- Racquet in front of you

- Head of the racquet in front of your face with the top of the racquet just below eye level

*Oops! Racquet head too low, must be held vertical
and in front of the chin/nose*

Get a grip

Two grips are appropriate for the forehand volley:
The Eastern forehand grip, often likened to a handshake, places your palm on the side of the racquet handle, parallel to the plane of your strings. This is the most natural grip position. However, it involves a slightly flexible wrist and is not ideal for the player who has difficulty keeping the racquet vertical. Players with strong wrists may use this, but the grip usually creates a racquet head that automatically drops, thus the need for a strong wrist.

Advantages of an Eastern grip:

- Easy to generate power

- Effective for beginners

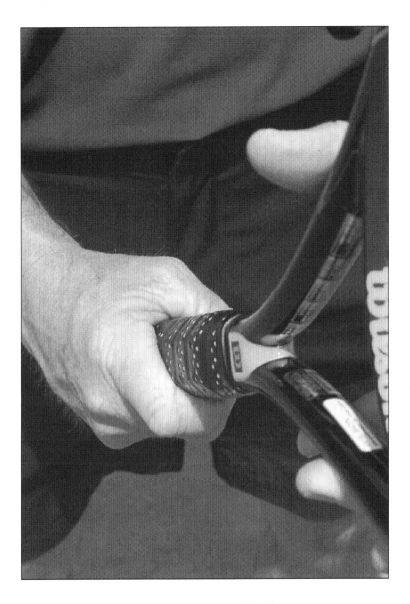

Eastern Forehand Grip
Palm on side of Racquet handle

The Continental grip places your palm somewhat on top of the racquet handle, about 45 degrees counter-clockwise from the Eastern. The Continental grip locks your wrist in place and should be used by players with "weak" wrists; it will aid your wrist to be strong, upward and locked.

Advantages of a Continental grip:

- No grip change needed when switching from forehand to back hand

- Low balls are easier because racquet head is more open

- Versatile

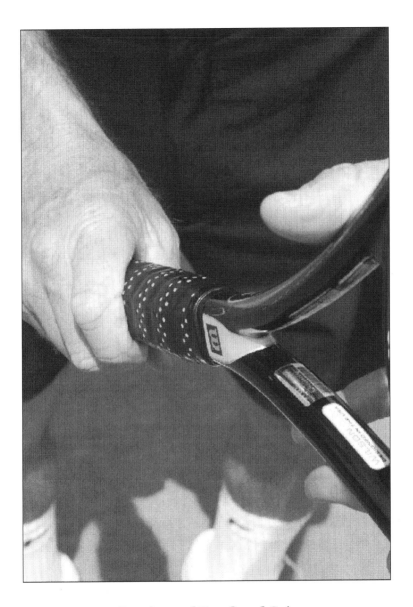

Continental Forehand Grip
Palm is somewhat on top of the Racquet handle,
about 45 degrees counter clockwise from the Eastern

On the other hand

Now that your racquet is on ready, you must turn so that you are square to the ball with the racquet up. Arms and wrists should almost be touching, as if you are handcuffed. You are now in a position to block the ball. As it approaches, the ball will be far enough away that you can meet it comfortably away from your body. The contact point is in front of your left leg for cross-court placement and a later contact for down the line. As you meet the ball, the non-dominant arm initially is out there as a guide, as a measuring device and as a third eye.

As you block the ball and stroke with your racquet, you have two choices with the non-dominant hand. It can stay and move forward or, for the most optimum power, it can go in the opposite direction. (See photo below.)

Advanced players can take the role of the non-dominant hand a step further, continuing to move it away from net as the racquet goes toward the net. The cross-over of the hands will give you plenty of pop and power. (Similar to karate drills for your arms and hands, the blending of both moving in tandem is what will make for an optimum shot)

Add an angle

When angling the ball, everything remains the same, the only difference being where the racquet meets the ball. In order to execute a cross-court (diagonal) shot, the racquet must meet the ball further out in front of your body. Both hands should move together, almost like a two-handed shot.

Tip:

Think about the surface area of the ball in terms of the back, left and right sides. As you focus on hitting the ball in front of your body, concentrate on the right side of the ball to hit an angle. Look directly at the contact area, keeping your eye on it as you watch the ball to the strings.

Walk the straight and narrow

For a straighter shot, think "Later, straighter." By meeting the ball a little later, but continuing to work both arms together, you will execute a straighter, less angled shot.

> **Tip:**
> *To hit the ball straight down the middle or down the line, focus on the back side of the ball, following it to the strings.*

Whether you are hitting straight or cross-court, your non-dominant hand should be very close to your racquet hand, as handcuffs would allow. The non-dominant hand should travel with the dominant hand in a short block.

Stay cool in the hot spot

The mid-court volley or hot spot volley (when your partner is receiving serve in the deuce court in doubles and you are awaiting their return by being positioned usually around the T on the ad side) is actually the tougher volley. If your partner hits a cross court return, you as a mid-court volleyer will then follow their return crosscourt to the net. But if the return is directed toward your opposing net player, you will have to stay set up and react. Whether it's a quick reaction or if you have time, the awareness of your non-dominant hand will help you make the best shot possible.

Ready position

In doubles, preparing for the mid-court volley means focusing on the opposing net player. When playing the deuce court, (your partner is receiving serve on the ad court) the right handed player should be turned in a backhand position near the T and staring at the net person. This shows the opponent that you are ready.

The opposite applies when you are playing the ad court. Face the opponent in a forehand stance. On either court, starting in a turned stance will give you a split-second advantage when the ball approaches. You are balanced and stable—prepared for either a forehand or backhand shot in the event your partner doesn't hit crosscourt.

Start with the head of the racquet up, see below picture position. At mid-court, expect to see a lot of low balls. They don't call it the hot spot for nothing!

On the other hand

For the beginning to intermediate level player, the handcuffed position is key for balance and measuring. The more advanced player will combine both arms and wrists moving simultaneously at the time the ball is contacted, but in opposite ways for the most optimum power.

Chapter 3

The Backhand Groundstroke

"The ball is coming to my backhand... Oh no! Maybe I'll run around it and hit a forehand instead." Sound familiar? If you lack confidence in your backhand, you're not alone. Many players find the backhand groundstroke more difficult to master than the forehand. Running around the backhand invites double trouble by exposing your weakness and by rendering you out of position for the next shot. With effective use of your non-dominant hand, you can develop a stronger, more controlled backhand, guaranteed to increase your confidence, improve your game and take your opponent by surprise. So what are you waiting for? Let's beef up your backhand.

Getting prepared

Since most players tend to favor the forehand, preparing to hit a backhand requires some adjustment. As soon as your brain registers, "backhand," you will most likely need to modify your grip. At the same time, you will be positioning your body to meet the ball—feet moving, shoulders turned and racquet arm back. As you align your right foot, right shoulder and right eye (for a right-handed player) the racquet head should be facing the back fence, butt cap facing the net.

The non-dominant hand plays an immediate and crucial role, adjusting the grip, cradling the racquet, aiding with the shoulder turn and racquet position. As you move to the area where you expect the ball to bounce, the non-dominant hand is like a holster. Unfortunately, on the backhand the non-dominant hand cannot serve its general purpose of measuring the distance to the ball. Learning to measure the backhand takes training and practice, while "the other hand" is busy performing other important tasks.

Swinging

For a flat or topspin backhand, your swing will be low to high. Ideally, the racquet head should start below the waist. The goal is to make the racquet head fairly flat on impact, slightly closed for topspin.

For a slice backhand, the racquet head starts above the ball, and the swing is high to low. In this case, the non-dominant hand helps bring the racquet up. If the ball bounces too high, the advanced player addresses the ball on the rise (before it reaches the full height of the bounce) to catch it at a comfortable height. You won't always be able to get in perfect position to hit the backhand groundstroke. By using the non-dominant hand in tandem with the racquet hand, you can still pull off a shot that keeps you in the point. As you stroke the ball, the non-dominant hand creates better balance and greater precision. For a solid, successful backhand, follow through with the racquet going forward and the non-dominant hand going back.

Using two hands

Are two hands better than one? Sometimes—and particularly on the backhand. There are several advantages to a two-handed backhand, and most players find it easier to learn than the one-handed version. Here's where your non-dominant hand really gets a chance to shine, by taking some of the work load off the racquet arm and providing that extra power and control. To execute a successful two-handed backhand, you have

three grip choices: Many beginners and some intermediate players choose to maintain the forehand grip with the racquet hand. In this case the racquet hand will have the softer grip as the non-dominant hand takes its position in the Western forehand grip and literally becomes the dominant hand. If you are ambidextrous or have a strong non-dominant hand, you might be successful. For a person with a weak non-dominant hand, this might be difficult.

A second choice of grip would be to change from the forehand Eastern grip to a Continental grip. By doing so, the non-dominant hand is on the racquet in a comfortable way—not loose, but not dominant. In this position, the two hands are working together, sharing the load 50/50.

The final option is to change the racquet hand grip to an Eastern backhand grip, giving it the stronghold. In this case, the non-dominant hand just goes along for the ride and can even let go right after contact.

Regardless of what grip combination you choose, the non-dominant hand will help with the follow-through, bringing the racquet up and around for the full impact of the stroke, ideally, touching the shoulder to the chin at the finish.

Chapter 4

The Backhand Volley

Many players consider the backhand volley one of the tougher shots to master. Whether you hit a one-or two-handed volley, the non-dominant hand becomes a crucial support. Once you master the technique, opponents expecting a weaker response from your backhand will be utterly surprised and dismayed. Let's explore some grip options and show you how to get the other hand involved to gain the power, control and confidence to make your backhand volley a secret weapon.

Be there and be square

Because the volley is hit from an up-close position (either mid-court or in the put-away area at the net), you have less time to get ready for the shot. Your initial stance will be neutral as you anticipate the volley, not knowing whether to expect it to your forehand or backhand. The racquet should be held at eye-level in a somewhat vertical position. As you recognize the direction the ball is coming, you must make an instant decision to turn the shoulders, perpendicular to the net and square to the ball. Even if you don't have time to turn the lower body, the upper body turn should be easy considering that the racquet shoulder is in the lead on the backhand volley.

A gripping decision

Although the volley can be played with either an Eastern or Continental grip, the best players typically choose the Continental grip for backhand volleys. With the Eastern grip, the strings are flatter, allowing you to meet the ball further out front, which helps generate power. The disadvantage? The Eastern grip necessitates a grip change from the forehand to backhand side which can be the split-second difference in meeting the ball in a position that allows you maximum power and control.

Continental Backhand Grip   *Eastern Backhand Grip*

By using the Continental grip from start to finish, no grip change is required. With this grip, you can choose to hit cross-court with slice, down the line or straight down the middle. But in order to make the straighter shots, you must meet the ball later to get power. This is why many less experienced, excited, energetic players prefer the Eastern grip. More advanced players develop the timing and patience to hold back a bit to make those "later, straighter" shots. The upper body turn should be easy considering that the racquet shoulder is in the lead on the backhand volley.

Regardless of which grip you choose, the non-dominant hand has a crucial job to do. Initially, the other hand helps cradle the racquet. On the way to the shoulder turn, it assists with the grip change. But that's just the beginning. Let's get into making the shot.

Delivering the one-two punch

The backhand volley is somewhat similar to the fore-hand volley in that it is not a swinging shot, but more of a punching action. As the ball comes to the position where you want to meet it, as you make contact with the ball, the racquet hand goes out toward the ball. As you block the ball with your racquet, shoulders stay aligned, the wrist stays firm and locked.

This is where the backhand volley takes on a different look from the forehand volley. Whereas the forehand calls for almost no follow through with the racquet, on the backhand volley, a bit of follow-through is allowed. The finish is similar to that of the backhand slice. Here again, what you do with the other hand is vitally important.

As you make that slight follow-through motion with the racquet hand, your non-dominant hand should move in the opposite direction, almost to a position of tautness as if pulling at the end of a string. Instead of trying to muscle the ball with the racquet hand alone, when the non-dominant hand does its job, you create a power zone and offensiveness that otherwise cannot be achieved.

Handling the high flyers and the low riders

When at the net, your opponent may attempt to lob over your head. A good lobber is likely to lob over your backhand side, expecting a weak response. For an effective return, address the shot as you would on a volley, with both arms working together (not just the racquet arm flicking) to keep you on balance and to get some power into the ball.

If your opponent takes the opposite tack and hits the ball toward your mid-section (your nose, tummy or between the legs), your backhand volley is the quickest, most effective defense. If you are caught facing the net with no time to turn, your racquet arm shoulder will allow you to act quickly to block the shot. Again, the non-dominant hand plays along to aid you with the block.

When it takes two hands

For players who wish to use both hands to execute the backhand volley, the non-dominant hand takes on an even more crucial role—actually becoming the dominant force. Here's how it works: Your racquet hand is at the bottom of the grip ready for a volley while the other hand is busy cradling the racquet at the throat. Once you see that the ball is coming to the backhand, you immediately turn, sliding the non-dominant hand down the racquet so that it is on top of the racquet hand.

If you are using the Continental grip with your racquet hand, slide the non-dominant hand down the racquet and use the Continental grip with it as well. By doing so, even when you are reaching desperately and letting go with the non-dominant hand, you will be able to meet the ball. To hit cross-court, you must meet the ball early. Remember: to go down the line, and sometimes straight ahead or down the middle, depending on where you are positioned, you must meet the ball later. In either case, the non-dominant hand has the workhorse grip and the racquet hand goes along for the ride.

Chapter 5

Serve, Overhand and Return of Serve

The Serve

Of all the shots in tennis, the serve is the only one that is all about you. It is the one shot that you and you alone generate and control. It is also the one shot that requires the most of your non-dominant hand. Perfect this shot and you will have an enormous advantage over any opponent.

Easier said than done, you're thinking. And you're right. Developing an effective serve takes constant practice. But once you get the hang of it, you'll see that it's like clockwork.

In this chapter, we'll explore the serve from toss to follow-through with emphasis on the starring role of the non-dominant hand.

Line it up

As with every stroke, getting your body in position is the first step to executing the perfect shot. When you're preparing to serve, you have time to line yourself up in the most ideal position—a luxury not afforded on any other shot. Take advantage of the time to set up physically and prepare mentally.

Setting up physically means positioning your feet at the baseline and aligning your body to your target. Think of the court like a clock. From the center of the net straight up is 12 o'clock. The baseline is 3 o'clock and the back fence is 6 o'clock.

When serving to the deuce court, your right leg will be slightly more open than when serving to the ad court. (Lefties must think counterclockwise in terms of a 10 to 11 o'clock stance.) Once your body is aligned, you are ready to start thinking about your serve.

Pictures showing body alignment, both arms upward, non-dominant tossing arm stays pointing towards 1-2 o'clock as you reach up with racquet arm to contact the ball. Prior to meeting the ball your N-D arm drops down and tucks into waist.

Perform your ritual

Proper execution of the serve requires concentration and a relaxed motion. To prepare mentally, most players develop a regular ritual or routine set of motions that they perform just prior to the serve. The purpose of the ritual is to get focused: study the opponent's service box, determine your target, breathe and get relaxed. Advanced players may also use this time to decide on grip position and what type of serve to deliver: flat, top spin or slice.

On the other hand

A typical ritual includes bouncing the ball a few times. And here's where your non-dominant hand goes to work. Ideally, you should bounce the ball along the 1 to 2 o'clock area of the court, getting focused on the contact zone.

It's a toss-up

The toss is the most critical element of a good serve, and the non-dominant hand holds the key to consistency.

When preparing to toss the ball for the serve, think of holding an ice cream cone between your thumb and first two fingers. If you hold on too tightly, you risk smashing it and making a drippy mess. Treat the tennis ball as if it is fragile, like an egg or a parakeet. You don't want to break it or smother it.

There are two basic methods of tossing the ball. The first and most popular method is to hold the ball loosely, palm up, and let go.

The second method is to hold the palm down with the back of the hand facing up. This position limits you from having the ball go anywhere other than straight up and straight in front of you, making the 2 o'clock position of the hand vital.

Regardless of which tossing method you use, it is important to have a loose arm—relaxed and extended as you release the ball. Ideally, it should be more like a lift than a throw, spin or toss, with the arm remaining in an upward, pointing position as the racquet arm comes out of its back-scratch position to strike the ball.

The non dominant arm, the tossing arm, is relaxed, extended and pointing, as it releases the ball.

As if the tossing motion were not enough responsibility for your non-dominant hand, prior to tossing, it must also cradle the racquet. This takes coordination and practice. As you begin your toss, holding the ball gently and cradling the racquet, the arms are once again working in tandem.

Tip

Practice tossing and serving under different conditions and learn to adjust accordingly for wind or sun. On a sunny day, practice using your non-dominant arm as a shade.

It takes two

Depending on your strategy, you must determine what kind of serve to deliver (flat, top spin or slice) and where to place the shot. Here again, your racquet arm plays its distinctive role. It must be relaxed (not stiff as on a volley), reaching and swinging freely with a final snap of the wrist. But it is the tandem motion of both arms that assures a fluid motion and propels the shot.

Deliver a flat out winner

To hit a flat serve, start with a Continental grip. As the racquet arm goes back into a back-scratch position, the non-dominant arm moves in tandem to toss the ball in front of your body to the right (2 o'clock). As your racquet arm uncoils, strike the ball with your palm facing out and follow through with the racquet across your body.

When the ball leaves the hand, in an extended racquet arm, but not so high that you have to stop and wait for it to come down. From beginning to end, the serve should be one fluid motion. At the same time you are striking the ball and following through with the racquet arm, the non-dominant hand crosses in the opposite direction, tucking into the body for maximum power. It is this duel motion that delivers the one-two punch.

N-D arm lifts, tosses, points and reaches

N-D arm points into the mid section after it lifts, tosses, points and reaches

Put a spin on it

To add slice to your serve, toss the ball slightly to the right, like peeling an orange. While sacrificing some power for the spin, an effective slice serve will have your opponent's head spinning as he or she scrambles to return it. That's when you go in for the kill!

On the other hand: The follow-through on the slice serve is similar to the flat serve, with the hands crossing and the non-dominant arm tucking into the body. The non-dominant hand must work even harder to do its part on the spin serve.

Top spin serve:

To add top spin or kick to your serve, adjust your toss to the left of 12 o'clock, more toward 10 or 11. By tossing to the left of center, the ball will be slightly behind your head but should still be into the court. As you swing the racquet, brush the left side and back of the ball. Racquet speed is essential to create the spin.

On the other hand: This time, the follow-through will be away from the body with the non-dominant hand working in tandem. Again, the non-dominant hand has to work very hard to add pop and power to your spin serve.

Serve up a winner every time

Whether you are playing singles or doubles, if you can serve down the T, in the middle of the two service boxes, you will have great success. The majority of players will move horizontally to return this serve, thus losing the ability to step into the ball. You may not have an ace, but you will put your opponent on the defensive and set yourself up for a potential winner on the next shot.

By delivering a top spin serve to the ad court or a slice to the deuce court, you can force your opponent off court to retrieve the ball, thus setting yourself up for the next shot. If you can hit the corner of the box or a couple of feet up, chances are your opponent will not be able to do much with the return. The better the level of play, the shorter you must hit the angle.

This is an effective strategy in both singles and doubles. Think of the serve as your best offensive weapon. Ace it and win the point outright or set yourself up for a winning shot off the return. The ball is in your court. Ready. Set. Serve!

The Overhead

You're at mid-court or at the net, anticipating a volley, when... oops! Here comes one of those giant, loopy lobs flying right over your head. What are you going to do? Turn and start shuffling! While your feet are busy getting you into position, your hands should be working in tandem, as if wearing handcuffs, for starters.

As the racquet arm goes up and into the back scratch position, the non-dominant arm points up toward the sky, ideally, to the right of center court. This is called the trophy position. The main function of the non-dominant arm is to point and scope out the ball, acting as a measuring device and aiding with balance as you prepare to strike.

As the racquet arm goes to the ball and you execute the shot, the non-dominant arm tucks into the body, just as it does on the serve.

By getting the non-dominant arm involved, you up your chances for hitting a consistent overhead with the power of the one-two punch. As a bonus, if it's "tricky" day, your non-dominant arm becomes a sun shield or a wind tracker.

Return of Serve

Returning the serve is one of the most important shots in the game. If you can't get the ball in play, you certainly can't win the point. The service return requires a quick decision and good reflexes. And as the serves come in faster, your return becomes a quicker, shorter swing rather than a regular groundstroke. If the ball comes really fast and you have little time to react, your return becomes more like a volley or block. The ready position for the return is the same for all players. Think of it as being in neutral gear as you anticipate the serve. The non-dominant hand cradles the racquet, helping hold the head steady, and preparing for a quick response.

Once you see what kind of serve is coming, you have only a split second to make a decision. Your brain must process your shot selection: Forehand or backhand? Low to high or high to low? Topspin or slice? Short block or long swing?

While your brain makes all the tough decisions, the non-dominant hand is busy getting your racquet out of neutral and revving up for action. From its cradling position, it immediately aids in the desired grip change, depending on the shot your mind has dictated the same functions as on your ground strokes and volleys, from meeting the ball to the follow through. Once the shot has been made, the non-dominant hand plays a key role in recovery and preparation for the next shot.

Remember, in the game of tennis, the non-dominant hand is juggling multiple jobs:

- Working as a measuring device

- Aiding with the grip

- Facilitating turn and torque

- Boosting your power

- Keeping your balance

- Preparing for the next shot

For maximum effectiveness on every shot, don't just let your non-dominant hand hang around. Give it a job, and start running up the score.

Appendix

Other Handy Tips

Adapt to Conditions

Your tennis performance on a given day is affected by many variables. The first and foremost is your opponent. You must respond to how he or she hits the ball and plan your strategy accordingly. You have a certain degree of control when it comes to action and reaction.

Other factors over which you have very little or no control include the court surface, the surroundings and the weather. While you may not be able to change these variables, you can learn to use them to your advantage. Many times, it's the small adjustments that lead to big results.

On the Surface

One of the most important variables that can significantly affect your game is the court surface, which can range from fast to slow. If you typically play on hard courts and find yourself on clay, or vice versa, you'll need to make some adjustments. Let's take a look at the most common court surfaces and how you can gain the competitive edge.

Clay courts

Clay courts are made of crushed shale, stone or brick, and are either red or green. The green Har-tru courts are most commonly seen in Clay courts are considered slow, because the balls bounce relatively high and more slowly, making it more difficult to hit an outright winner. The softer surface absorbs power as well as shock to the body, making it the surface of choice for many older players or players with knee or back issues. But that doesn't mean it's a powder puff game.

Points are generally longer, requiring a high degree of overall fitness and stamina. Sometimes the underdog will have the advantage, if he or she is fit and patient. Statistics show that more upsets occur on clay than on hard surfaces. This could be good news if you are the weaker player. But if you have the stronger game, be wary of the opponent who seeks to simply wear you down. On clay, it is particularly important to take your time on the point and wait for the opportunity to put the ball away.

If you are a player who relies on big serves to win, you may find clay a less effective surface for that game, because the surface absorbs the power and slows the ball down. Your best bet to win is to develop a consistent baseline game and to play defensively. Because of the irregular surface, bounces can be tricky, requiring greater focus and more patience than might be necessary on a faster court. Topspin and slice are very effective on clay as these shots bite into the surface. For the same reason, drop shots can be downright deadly.

Movement on clay courts is different from other surface in that the feet don't have a solid grip. Playing on clay often involves the ability to slide into the ball during the stroke, as opposed to running and stopping like on a hard or grass court. Your shoes can make a big difference in your ability to move effectively on clay. If you are not accustomed to playing on clay, make it a point to practice on the surface prior to a match or tournament.

Sidebar:
Slow Court Tactics
• Get fit: Endurance is the name of the game on a slow court. (See Appendix B for endurance training tips.)

• Choose the right shoes: Don't go slip-sliding away. Stay in control with the right soles.

• Be patient: Outright winners aren't as easy to come by on a surface such as clay. Slow and steady wins the race.

Incorporate topspin and slice

• Topspin will kick up and slice will stay down as these shots bite into the soft surface.

• Use your drop shot: This shot will die faster on a soft surface, and will likely leave your opponent little choice but to say, "Good shot," possibly followed by a mumbled expletive.

Hard courts

Hard courts are generally made of cement or plastic. Depending on the thickness and composition of the top surface, they can vary in speed from medium to fast. In general, they are faster than clay but slower than grass. Because the surface is solid and firm, hard courts provide the truest, most predictable bounces, serving to equalize various playing styles.

This is the time to show off your serve, as opponents will have less time to react to the fast bounce. A serve and volley strategy can also be highly effective. While topspin and slice have their place in the hard court game, powerful flat balls are best.

Grass courts

Grass courts are the fastest courts of all. They consist of grass grown on very hard-packed soil, similar to golf greens. Bounces depend on how healthy the grass is, how recently it has been mowed, and the wear and tear of recent play. Because the surface is less firm than hard courts, the ball bounces lower so that players must reach the ball faster. Points are usually very short and the serve plays a crucial role. If you are a serve and volley player, you'll have a distinct advantage on grass. By getting into the net and cutting off the return, you take control of the point and will often be in position to hit an outright winner.

Sidebar

Fast Court Tactics

• Attack: Fast courts make for fast points. This is not the time to sit back and wait for your opponent to make a mistake. Force the point by aggressively attacking.

• Choose the right shoes: Don't break your neck (or anything else) by wearing the wrong shoes.

• Go for the big serve: Big serves are ideal for fast courts. Your opponent will barely see it, much less have time to return it.

• Approach the net: Rallying from the baseline is not the best strategy on a fast court. Get to the net! Serve and volley; chip and charge.

• Keep the ball low: Don't set your opponent up for the perfect volley or overhead smash. By keeping the ball down, you force your opponent to hit up, allowing you to get to the net and put it away.

• Prepare early: Because you have less time to set up for your shot, you may need to shorten your backswing and hit from an open stance.

• Stay deep on the return: Expect serves to come in hard and fast. Stand a little deeper to allow for reaction time.

Indoor courts

Indoor courts can be made of wood, cement or Astroturf, which is a carpet-like material. Carpet-style indoor courts are the most common, and are generally fairly fast, although not as fast as grass. Cement indoor courts play similarly to hard courts. Wood courts are the least common and tend to play fast as well. Newer technologies include vinyl and other fabrications which can mimic the speed of various other court surfaces. If you will be playing an indoor tournament, try to practice on the court and get a feel for the surface so that you can adjust your game accordingly.

Other Conditions and Distractions

In addition to the court surface, many other conditions can affect your game: wind, sun, noise and your audience, to name a few. To play your best, you need to develop specific strategies, both physical and mental, to overcome the small aggravations that can make or break your game.

Riding the wind

When playing outdoors, the wind can be one of the trickiest obstacles to overcome. With practice, you can make the wind your friend or at least, learn to get along. First, determine the direction of the wind. If there is no obvious pattern, pick up a leaf or straw or some other debris from the court and toss it in the air. Now you should have a better idea of what the wind might do to the ball.

Since you will have to play the wind from both sides of the court, you need to adjust your mindset on each changeover. For example, when playing against the wind, you can swing harder and be more aggressive, knowing that the wind will reign in your shot and keep the ball inside the court. On the other hand, when playing with the wind, you may need to practice more restraint on your swing, staying more focused and keeping control.

When the wind is blowing parallel to the net, you must adjust your shot selection and aim accordingly. If you see that every cross-court shot you hit is landing mid-court instead, you will need to increase the angle to overcome the effects of the wind. If the wind is blowing your cross court shot into the side fence, you should aim more toward the middle and let the wind carry it the rest of the way.

Whichever way the wind may blow, it is likely to affect your serve. Adjust by keeping the toss lower. Lobs can also be unpredictable and dangerous when hitting against the wind. You know what happens when the ball doesn't quite make it high enough to clear your opponent's reach... Unless you want to eat that ball (or obtain a new navel), better keep it closer to earth than the moon.

Your best strategy on a windy day is a full arsenal of shots and styles mixed with a generous amount of patience. Practice on windy days so that you are better prepared for a blustery match.

Oh say, can you see?

Sun can also be a major factor when playing outdoors, particularly on the serve, the overhead and the high volley. The sun typically affects one side of the court more than the other, and it is essential to practice from both sides. You can learn to adjust your toss and alter your swing so that you are not looking directly into the sun. You can also save your eyes from the glare by wearing a hat or visor and/or sunglasses. If you are uncomfortable wearing a hat or glasses, the next best sun defense is your non-dominant hand.

(See page 69 for a demonstration on how to shield your eyes without sacrificing the shot.)

You can run, but you can't hide

You might be thinking that if outdoors is so treacherous, why not just take the game inside? Playing indoors may or may not be any better when it comes to battling court conditions. Minus the wind and sun, indoor courts have their own set of obstacles and distractions. Compared to the wide-open sky, the ceiling can make you feel a bit claustrophobic. It presents a different view on the serve and overhead and may even get in the way of a high lob.

Just as it is outdoors, sometimes the temperature is uncomfortable. A too-hot, stuffy indoor environment can be even more unpleasant than a hot, sunny day outside. While not like looking into full sun, indoor lights can be tricky, as well. So what's a player to do? If at all possible, practice in the facility before playing a match to familiarize yourself with the specific quirks of the surface and the structure. If you do not have the opportunity to practice, you must use your powers of concentration and try to tune out every distraction. As you warm up for the match, focus on the ball and tune out your surroundings.

Breaking the sound barrier

Have you ever gone up for the toss on your serve, only to hear a distant horn or a barking dog, throwing you completely off and causing you to fault? As unfair as it may seem, no one can control what goes on beyond the fence or stadium. What you can learn to control is your reaction to the distraction. Indoors or out, you may be distracted by any number of noises, from a bird cawing to a blaring siren. Even generic crowd noise or well-meaning fans cheering on the sidelines can inter-fere with your concentration. Train your ears to tune out extraneous noise by focusing on the sound and the rhythm of the ball.

For your best performance, you must learn to tune out the annoyances and tune in to the task at hand.

Get Fit

As a tennis player, you know how important it is to have the right shoes and the right racquet. But when it comes to the playing the game, no amount of air in your soles or titanium in your frame can win a match.

There simply is no substitute for a fit, lean body. And since you can't go to the store and buy a new one, your best strategy is to keep yours in tip-top shape.

Tennis requires a specific set of physical skills, including speed, endurance, strength and agility. While playing the game is great exercise in itself and on-court practice is key to your success as a player, some specific off-court preparation can improve your game and help ward off injuries.

Whether you are a weekend warrior, tournament player or pro, you can benefit from a sport-specific fitness routine consisting of cardiovascular training, strength training and stretching. Short of hiring a professional trainer to develop a program for you, here are some suggestions for keeping your body in winning condition:

Cardio Training

Want to improve your speed, endurance and reaction time? Get your heart pumping. Since most of your play will be outdoors, exercise outside whenever possible. Biking, inline skating, brisk walking and swimming are excellent endurance activities that are easy on the joints. When the weather forces you indoors, head to the gym and go for the Stairmaster or elliptical. While a short jog can provide good cardio training and is especially valuable as a warm-up activity, generally speaking, tennis players should avoid long-distance running. Your body gets enough pounding on court. Save your running for drills: sprints (uphill sprints are particularly effective), interval running and diagonal shuffle steps, which are ideal choices for improving your speed and agility on court. If a nearby tennis facility offers cardio tennis, sign up. These fast-paced drill sessions are ideal for improving your overall fitness level, coordination and reaction time.

Strength Training

While it is important to develop muscular strength, too much muscle mass can slow you down on court. Still, the right kind and right amount of resistance training or weight training can benefit your game in several ways. Not only can it help you develop the strength needed to produce more powerful strokes, but it will help reduce body fat and boost your metabolism, in turn, helping you gain even greater speed and endurance.

If you are hitting the gym or working with a trainer, remember, the goal is strength without bulk. You can achieve this by combining higher repetition with lighter weights. An alternative is to simply use your own body weight as your resistance. Pushups and pullups are perfect exercises for adding power to your strokes. Abdominal crunches are essential for core strength and stability.

Stretching

In addition to stamina and strength, tennis also requires a full range of motion, making gentle stretching a vital component of your fitness program. The best stretching program for tennis players incorporates two kinds of stretching: dynamic and static, but it is important to know what to do when. Dynamic stretches are moving stretches, best for warming up, while static stretches consist of stretching a muscle (or a group of muscles) to its farthest point and then holding that position for 15-30 seconds, most appropriate for cooling down and for lengthening muscles between matches.

Tip: Recommended stretching sequence
• Warm up (five minutes brisk walking or light jogging to break a light sweat)
• Dynamic stretches (several repetitions of tennis-specific movements)
• Tennis play or training
• Static stretches
• Dynamic Stretches

Dynamic stretches should mimic the movements of your sport.

Following are some suggested dynamic stretches for tennis players:

Quick Kicks
Lightly jogging, bring heels up to buttocks rapidly. (Avoid this exercise if you have knee problems.)

High step trunk rotations
Bring your right knee up high while rotating your trunk to the right (don't hold the stretch). Switch legs and repeat, rotating your trunk to the left.

Front lunge

Planting one foot, take a long step forward with the opposite leg and move into a quarter squat and hold for two seconds, keeping the front knee aligned with the ankle. Switch legs and repeat.

Crossover lunge

Planting one foot, take a wide step across your body and slightly forward with the opposite leg and move into a quarter squat. Switch legs and repeat.

Side lunge

Planting one foot, take a wide step out to the side with the opposite leg and move into a quarter squat. Switch legs and repeat.

Waist bends

Feet forward. Keep knees, heels and calves lined up straight. Put up both arms like you are going to block somebody. Bend at the waist, slowly right and left. Working upper torso.

Arm circles

Circle arms, 10 large and 10 small, each way, then shadow swing, practicing the motion of each stroke, including serves and overheads with follow-through.

Other helpful stretches

Wrist rotations, finger curls and head rolls.

Static Stretches

Static stretching is not recommended just prior to a match. In fact, research indicates that power and strength are temporarily reduced immediately after static stretching. But that doesn't mean you should skip it altogether. Static stretches should be performed after the activity, when your blood is flowing and your muscles are loose. This not only helps elongate muscles, but also decreases stiffness and soreness and speeds recovery time. Static stretching is also effective between matches to maintain flexibility and prevent injury. Pay particular attention to potential trouble spots, which include the hamstrings, lower back, After play, perform three to five static stretches, held for 15 to 30 seconds, for each muscle group. Stretch until you feel gentle tension in the muscle, never to the point of pain.

If yoga classes are available in your area, consider joining a class. The practice of yoga not only helps increase range of motion and flexibility, but also improves mental focus and balance.

Tip: Be sure to warm up with a brisk walk or light jog before attempting any stretching exercise.

Winning nutritional strategies

Just as your car won't run without gas, your body cannot operate properly without the right fuel. The nutritional choices you make before stepping onto the tennis court can have a tremendous effect on your performance.

This includes your daily diet as well as what you eat just prior to a match. Following are some nutritional strategies to help you play your best game:

Aim for your optimal weight. If you are dragging around extra pounds, chances are you are not moving as fast as you could be on the tennis court. Trim down the fat and see a noticeable improvement in your game.

On the other hand, if you are skin and bones, you may need to put on some muscle to improve your performance. Avoid highly processed foods and junk food, high-fructose corn syrup and excessive sugar, even when trying to gain weight.

Make carbs count. Many people have come to think of carbohydrates as enemies. In fact, if you are an athlete, carbs are your best friends, providing the primary fuel for muscles. Without enough, you are likely to run out of steam. Depending on your activity level, aim to have six to eight servings (one serving is equal to one-half cup cooked pasta or one slice of bread) of foods such as pasta, wheat bread, whole grain cereals, brown rice, potatoes, yams, sweet potatoes and vegetables each day.

Power up on protein. Protein is also vital to your strength and stamina. Ideally, about one-third of each meal should come from protein such as turkey, chicken, fish, eggs, lean cuts of beef, tofu and low fat dairy products.

Choose healthy sources of fat. Nuts, avocado and cold water fish are good sources of the kind of fat that is beneficial, not harmful, to the body.

Get hooked on fiber. Consume 25 to 35 grams of fiber per day. High fiber foods include whole grains, vegetables, fruits, and cereals. Read labels and be aware of fiber content in everything you eat.

Keep hydrated. Drink plenty of water to maintain hydration while training. Avoid sugary drinks such as sodas, juice or lemonade. Although these may contain water and some carbohydrates, they also contain sucrose or fructose, which can ultimately lead to gastrointestinal distress and decreased performance. Take a multivitamin/mineral supplement daily.

Eat to win

Before a match, you will want to eat a meal which releases glucose into the body slowly without an insulin surge. A pre-match meal should include foods with a low glycemic index. (The glycemic index (GI) is a method of classifying foods based on their acute glycemic impact.) Foods that are digested quickly, appear in the bloodstream quickly, and raise blood sugar and insulin concentrations quickly, have a high GI. Foods that take longer to digest have a low GI. For a list of appropriate low-GI foods, visit www.the-gi-diet.org/lowgifoods (http://www.the-gi-diet.org/lowgifoods).

After your match, the most important nutrient to replace is water. Don't rely on thirst. In fact, if you are thirsty, you are already slightly dehydrated. Drink plenty of water before, during and after a match or training session.

Electrolytes such as potassium and sodium must also be replenished after a match. Try foods rich in sodium (pretzels, crackers, cheese) and potassium (potatoes, bananas, orange juice).

To ensure adequate muscle recovery, within the first hour after exercise, you should eat to replenish your carbohydrates. This is when you can choose high GI foods, such as bread, graham crackers, corn chips, carrots, potatoes, rice or rice cakes, waffles, plain bagels, and watermelon. A serving of protein is also recommended.

Drink to your health
Hydration before, during and after exercise is an important component to your performance. While individual fluid intake needs vary, you can use the following guidelines as a starting point and modify according to your needs.

Hydration before Exercise
• Drink about 15-20 fl oz, 2-3 hours before exercise
• Drink 8-10 fl oz 10-15 min before exercise

Hydration during Exercise

• Drink 8-10 fl oz every 10-15 min during exercise
• If exercising longer than 90 minutes, drink 8-10 fl oz of a sports drink (with no more than 8 percent carbohydrate) every 15-30 minutes.

Hydration after Exercise
• Weigh yourself before and after exercise and replace fluid losses.
• Drink 20-24 fl oz water for every 1 lb lost.
• Consume a 4:1 ratio of carbohydrate to protein within the 2 hours after exercise to replenish glycogen stores.

Source: *Consensus Statement of the 1st International Exercise-Associated Hyponatremia Consensus Development Conference, Cape Town, South Africa 2005. Clinical Journal of Sport Medicine. 15(4):208-213, July 2005.*